Editor: Dominique Boudet, Paris

Graphic design: Ruedi Baur, Paris

Layout: Odyssée Khorsandian, Paris

Photography: Marco Cappelletti, Venise

Post-production: Filippo Rossi, Alessio Tamborini

Translation (French–English): Kiel Bonhomme

Proofreading: Joëlle Bibas, Lisa Schons

Pre-press, printing, binding:
DZA Druckerei zu Altenburg GmbH, Thuringia

Park Books
Niederdorfstrasse 54
8001 Zurich
Switzerland
www.park-books.com

Park Books is being supported by the Federal Office of Culture with a general subsidy for the years 2016-2020.

ISBN 978-3-03860-213-2

OMA – Toulouse Exhibition and Convention Center

PARK BOOKS

Dominique Boudet, ed.
Marco Cappelletti, photography
Ruedi Baur, graphic design

CÉDEZ LE
PASSAGE

BANDES
RUGUEUSES
70

PARC DES EXPOSITIONS
CENTRE DE CONVENTIONS
Accès Exposants 2
Accès Public
Accès Exposants 2

MET-SI 13
MET-SI 20

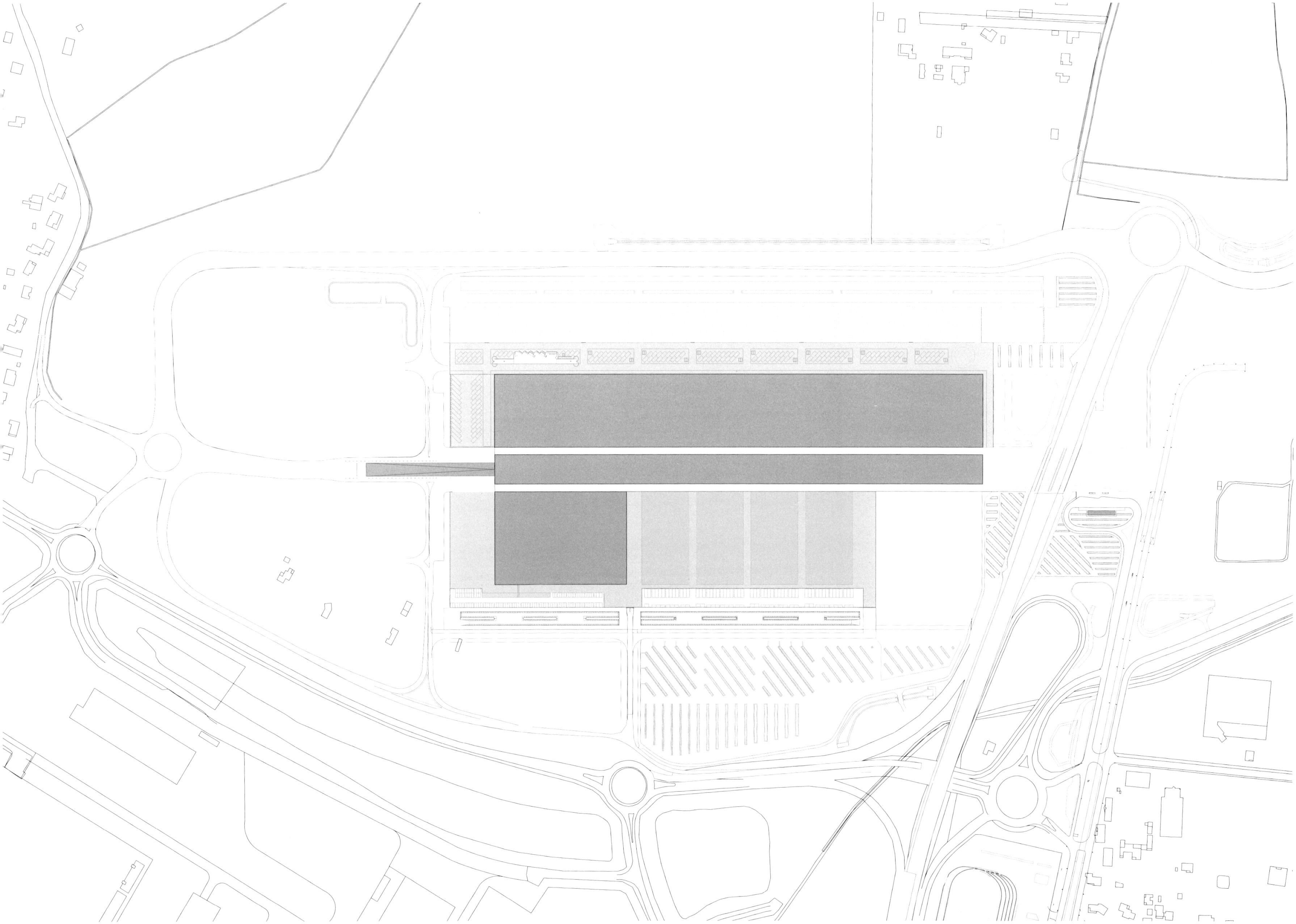

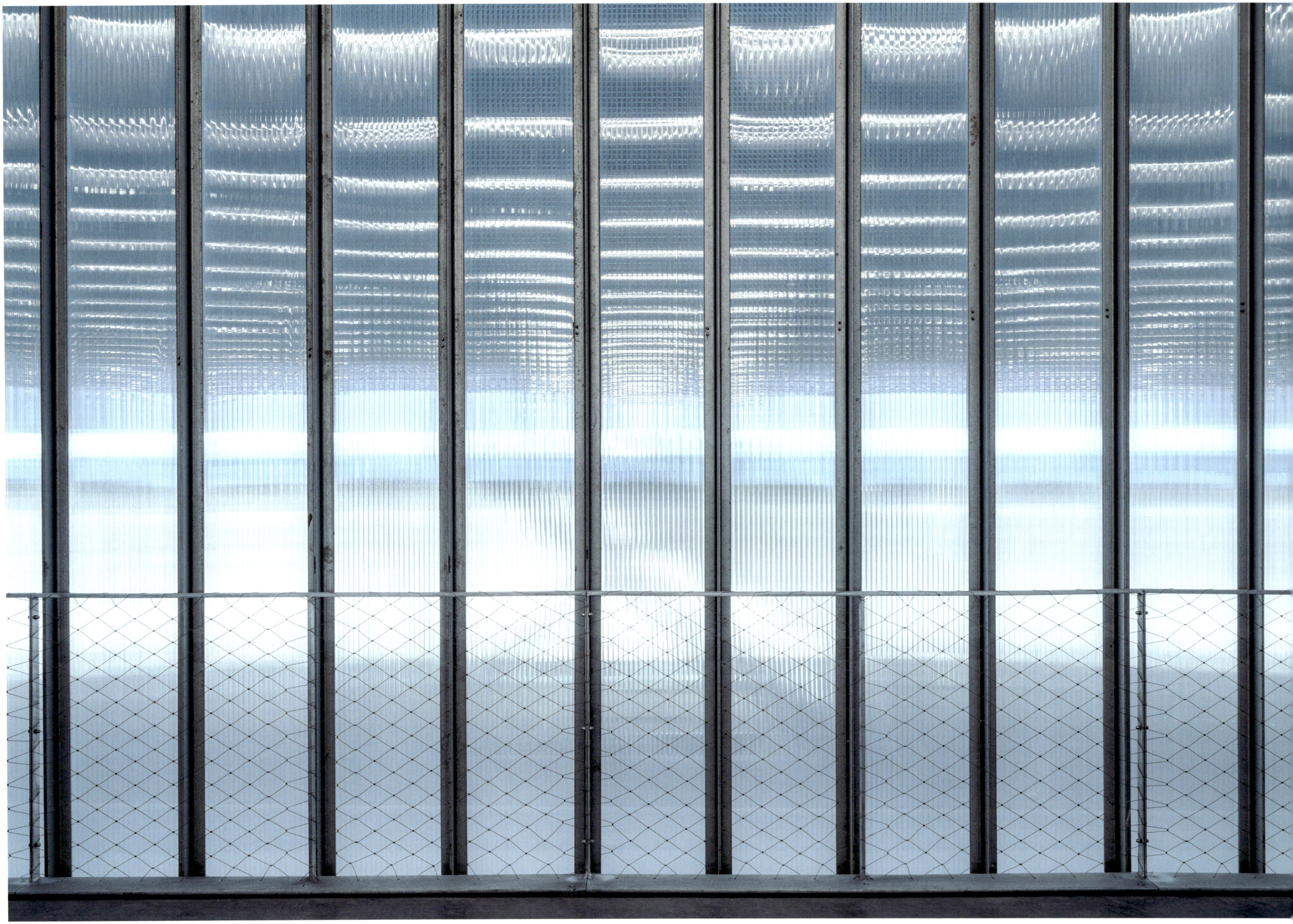

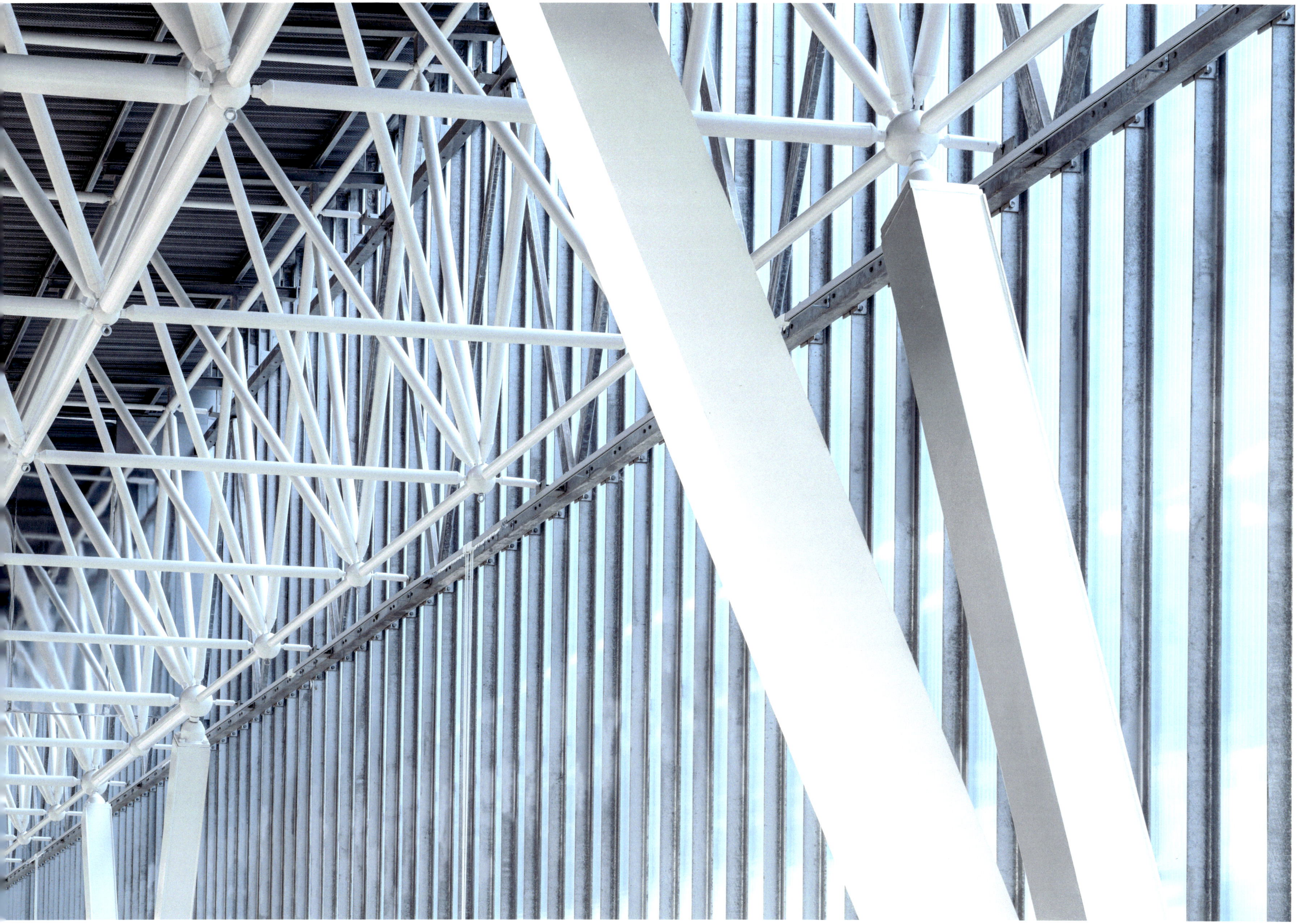

1

HALL
1
2-7↓
P
A-Z↓

HALL
6

HALL
2
P
M-Z →

8
P

8
P

1

6

HALL
8
P

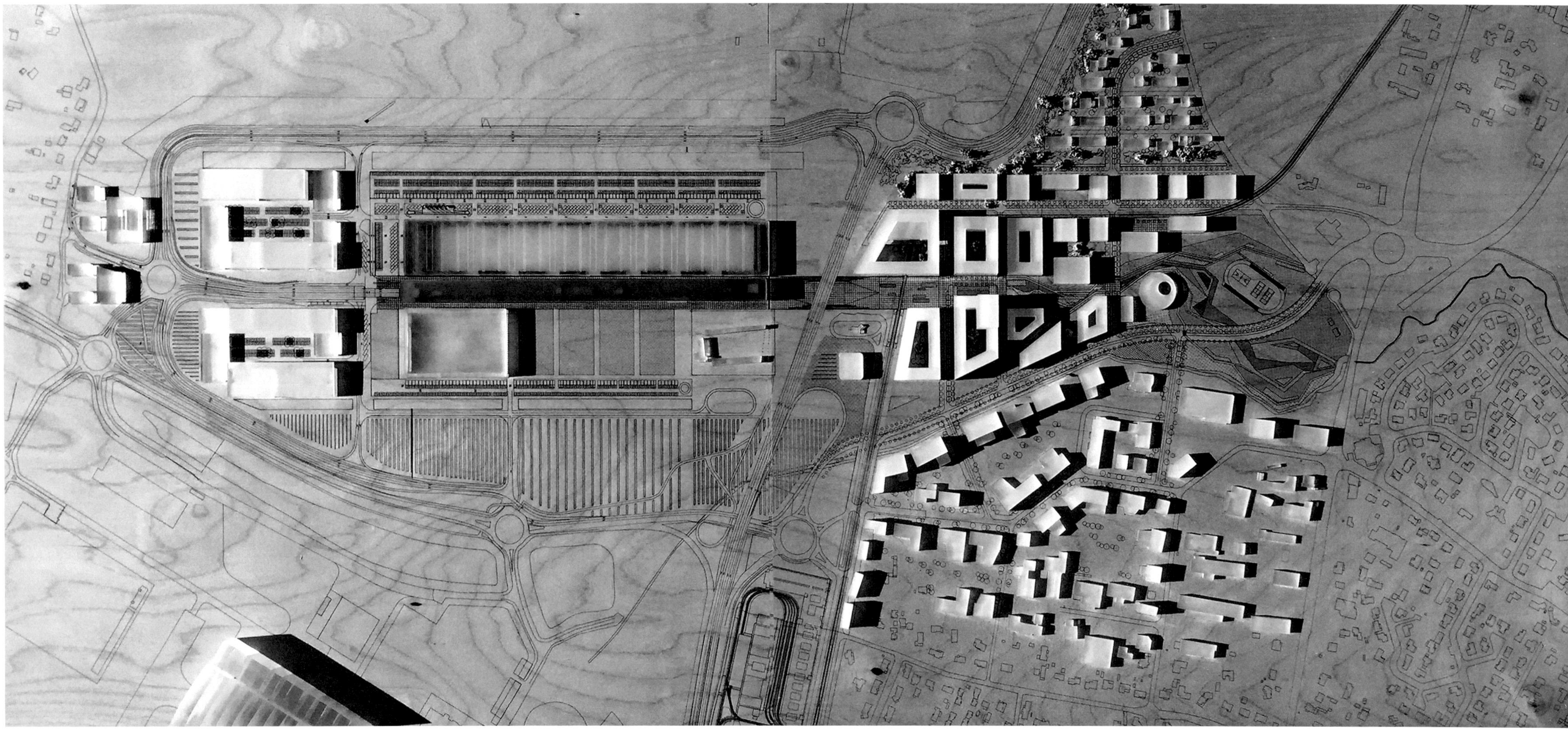

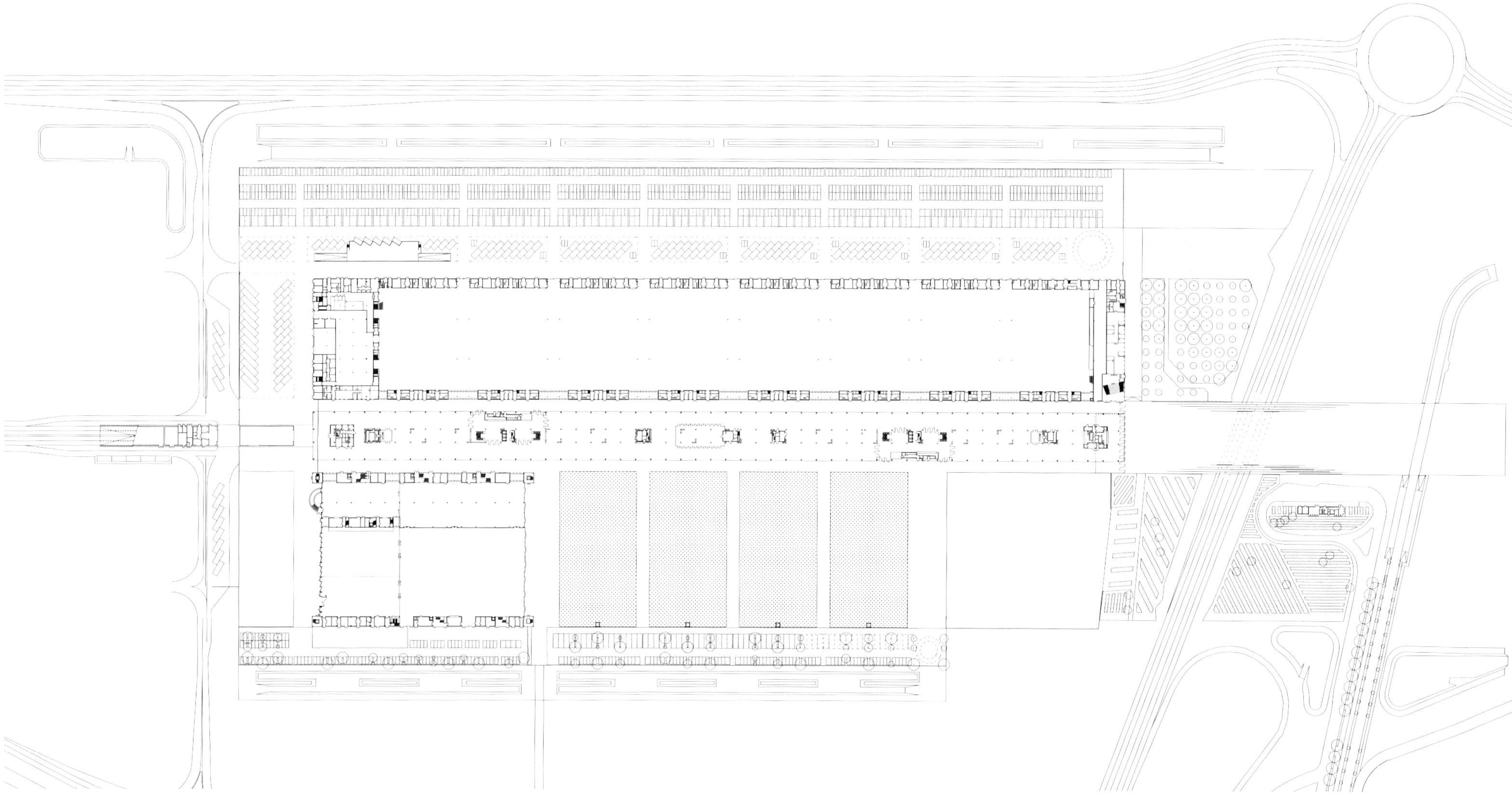

Exhibition hall, roof level

Exhibition hall, mezzanine level

Exhibition hall, ground-floor level

Scale 1:500

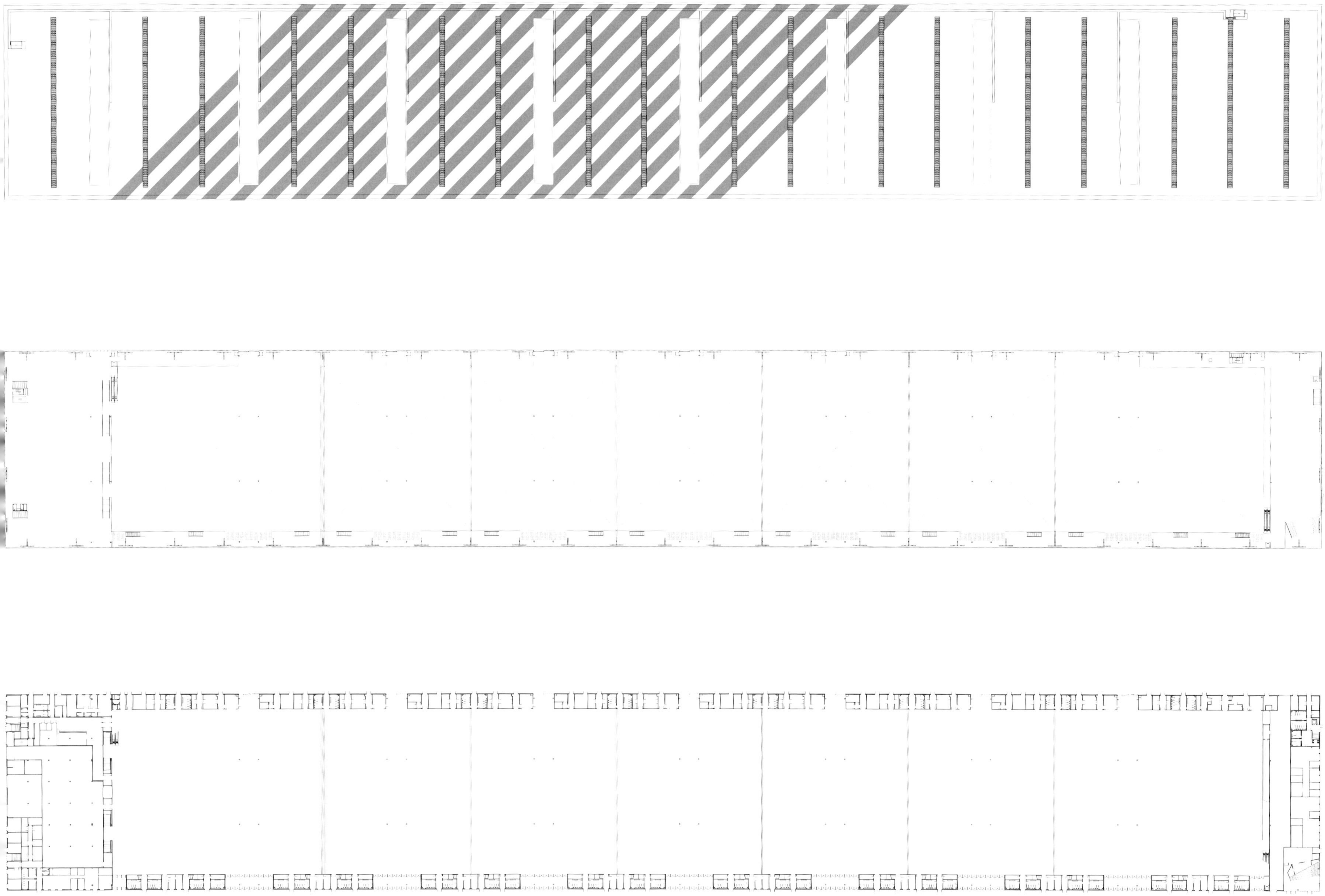

1

Exhibition hall, east and north façades

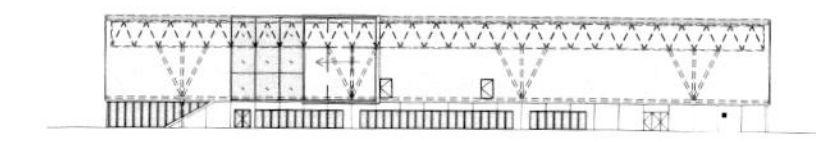

Exhibition hall, west and south façades

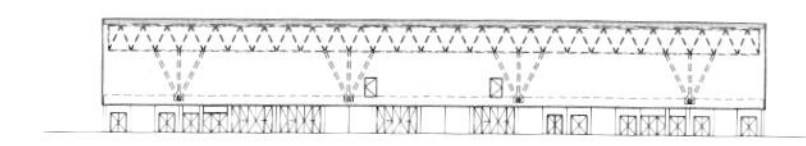

Exhibition hall, cross and longitudinal sections

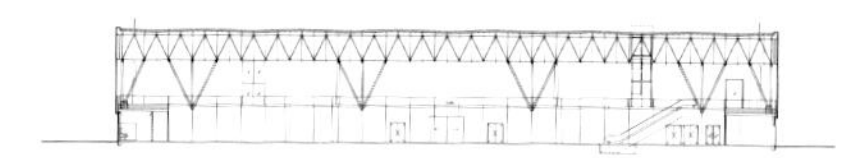

Scale 1:500

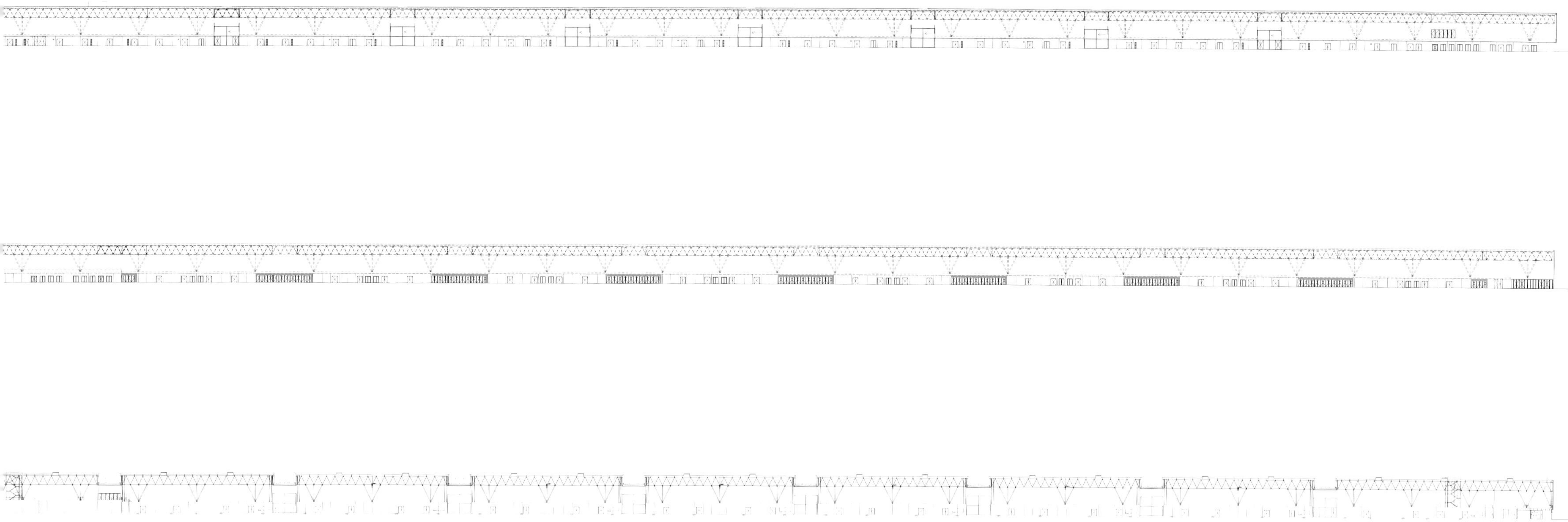

Silo car park, level 5

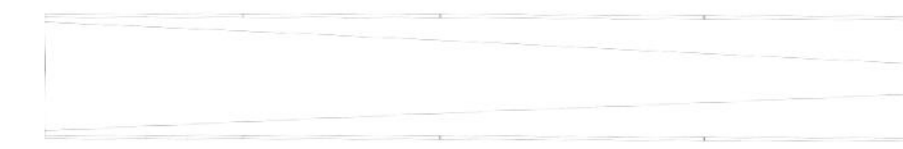

Silo car park, level 4

Silo car park, level 3

Silo car park, level 2

Silo car park, ground-floor level

Scale 1:500

Silo car park, west and south façades

Silo car park, cross and longitudinal sections

Silo car park, cross and longitudinal sections

Silo car park, east and north façades

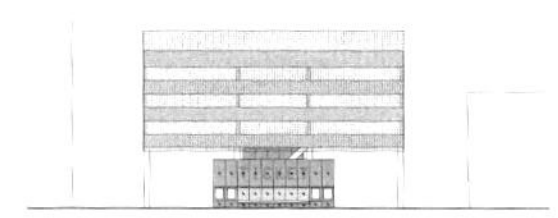

Scale 1:500

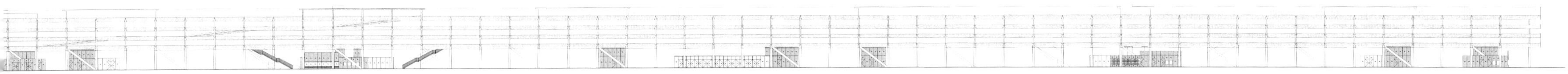

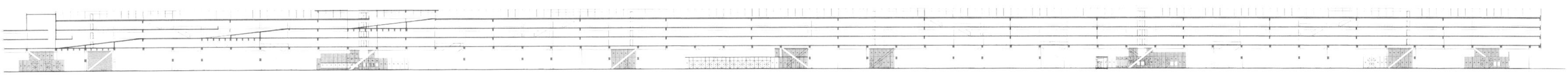

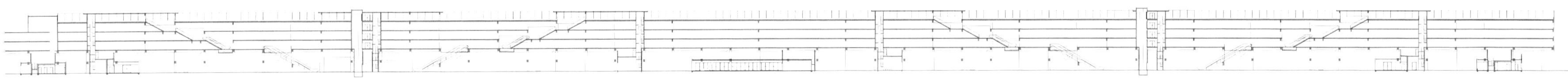

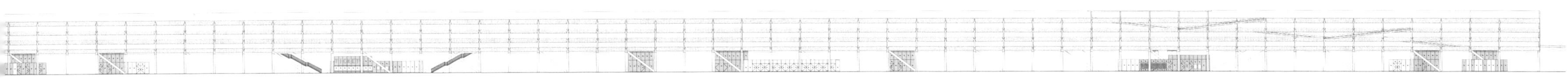

Convention center, cross section

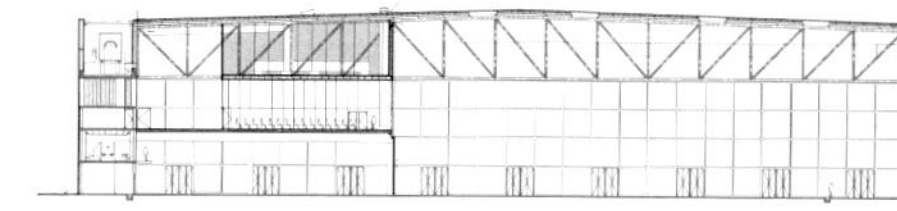

Convention center, longitudinal section

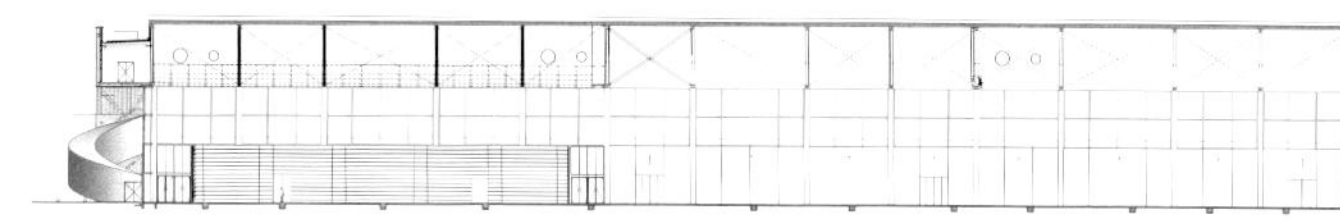

Convention center, east and north façades

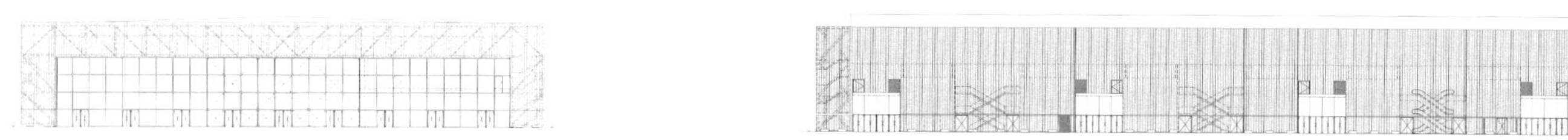

Convention center, west and south façades

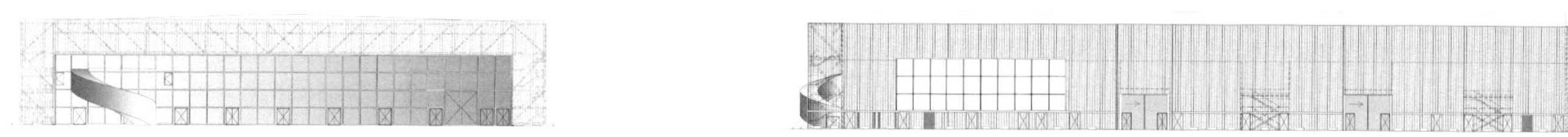

Scale 1:500

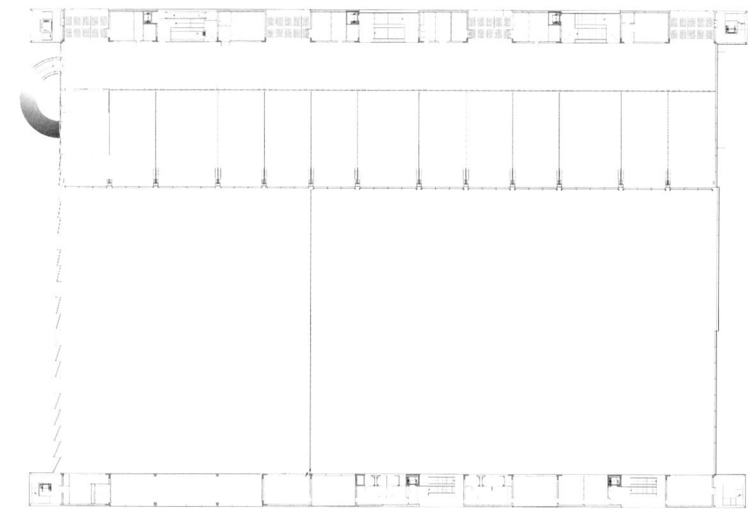

Convention center, meeting-rooms level

Convention center, ground-floor level

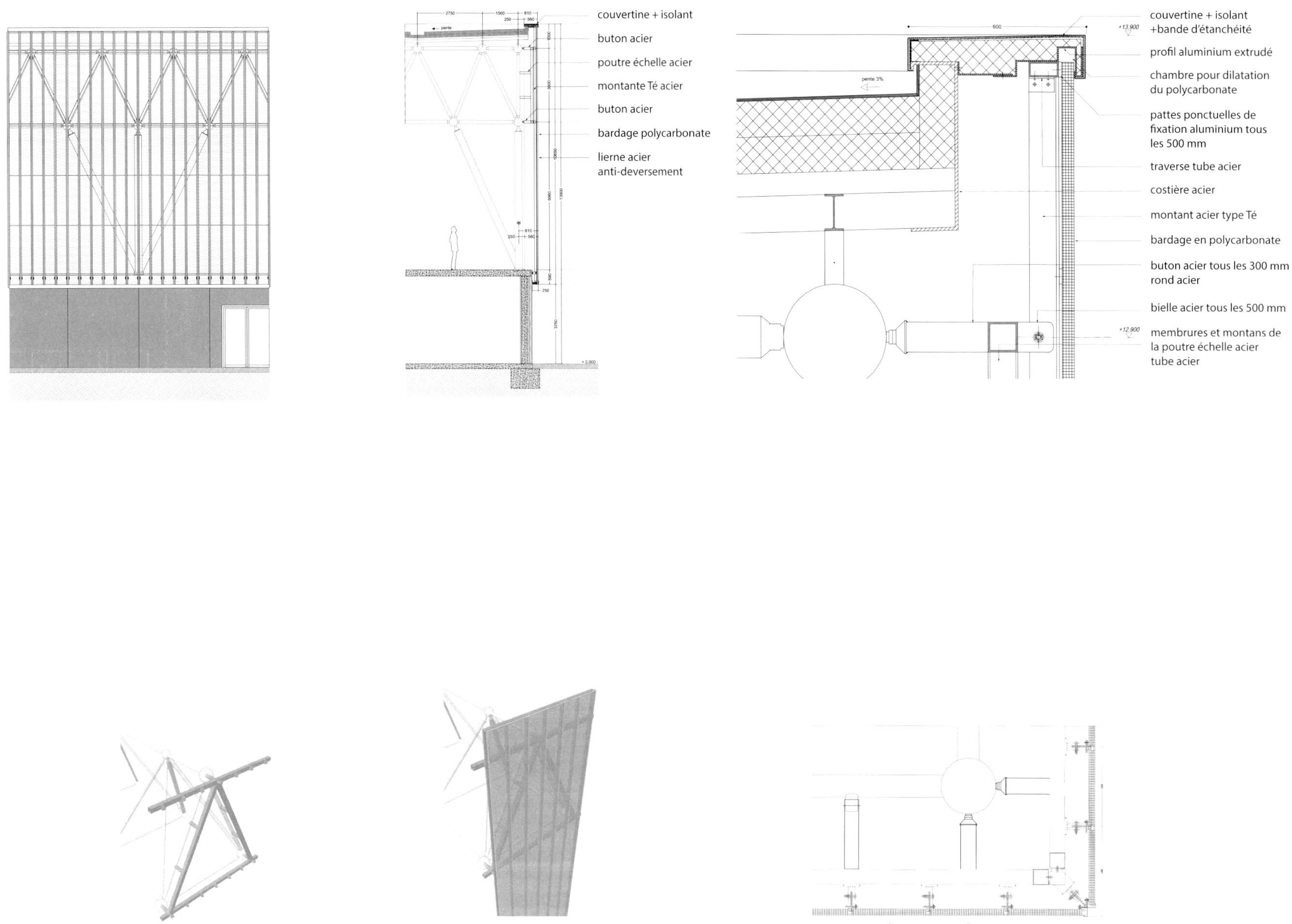

Exhibition hall, sections on façade

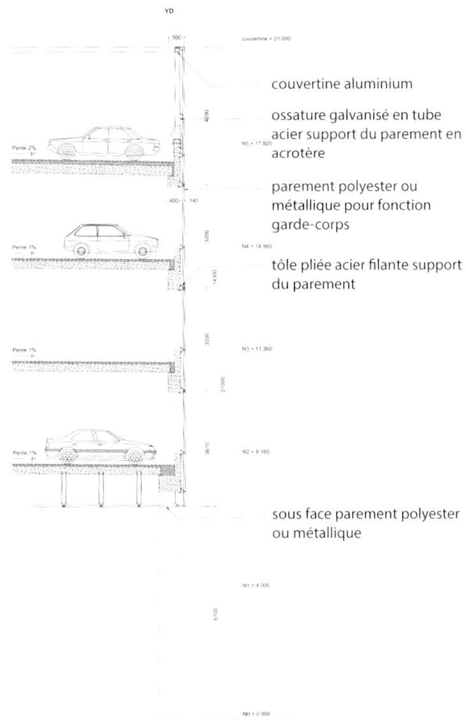

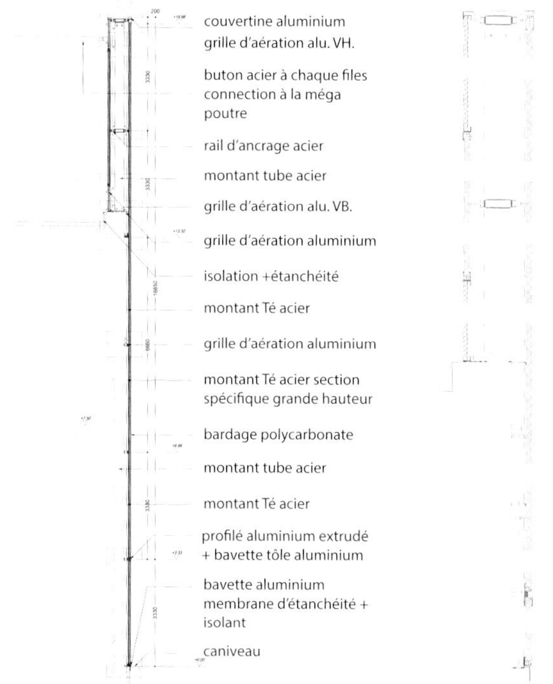

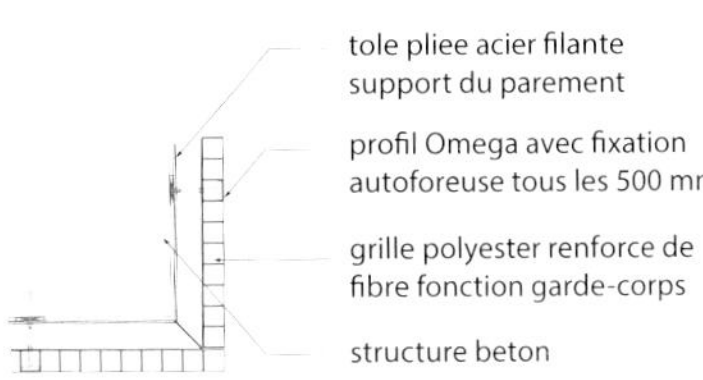

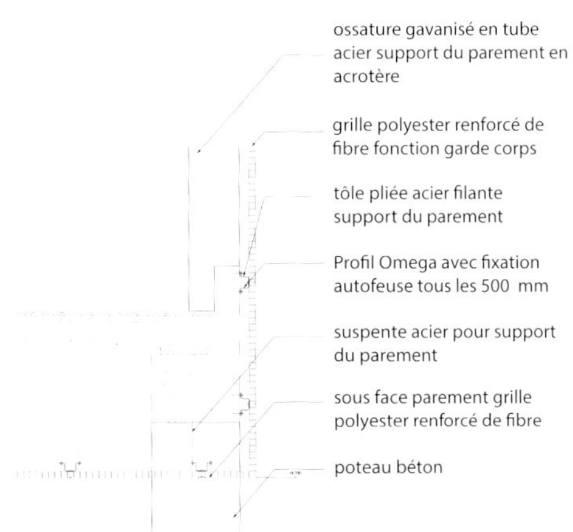

Silo car park, sections on façade

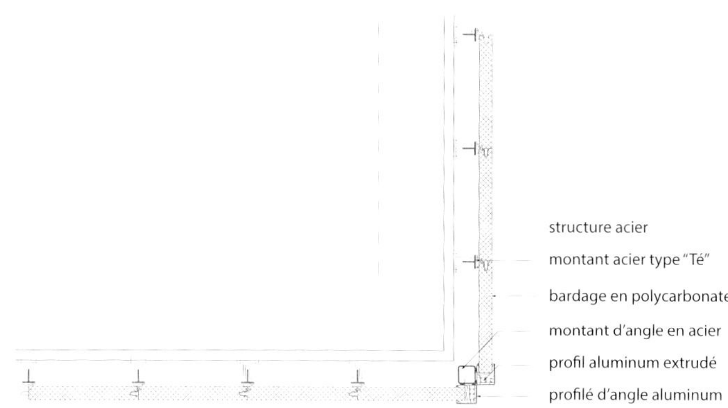

Convention center, sections on façade

rom Territory to Architecture and *Vice Versa*

ominique Boudet

ong volumes with pure forms draw a clear line in the ountryside. On the outskirts of the city, such is the pparition of the MEETT, Toulouse's new exhibition and onvention center. Designed by Dutch agency OMA, this uropean-scale facility meets the two objectives set by rance's fourth-largest urban metropolis in embarking n this major investment: developing the infrastructure hat enables it to host major professional, cultural and porting events, and reinforce an economic hub to the orth-west of the city.

n response to the multiple challenges posed by the stablishment of such an important infrastructure on a ensitive site (a nearly untouched rural landscape), OMA roposed facilities that are spectacular in their dimen-on, 565m long, 225m wide, yet simple in their organi-ation, three minimalist volumes juxtaposed in parallel, nd formidable in their efficiency. All of the architec-ure's elements balance the synergies of its environ-nental impact, functionality, architecture, and urban ootprint.

n essential element of the facilities: a silo car park, a ng piece of infrastructure replacing the common out-oor parking area, the customary plague of large facili-es whose size requires being located on the periphery f the urban sphere. The environmental gain is evident: ninimized use of terrain instead of the tens of hectares itially planned for parking. The functional advantage no less significant: placed in the heart of the facilities, puts visitors in direct and immediate contact with the xhibition halls or convention center. The silo car park ansforms the operation and performance of the entire te. As a compact unit, the MEETT is a machine for mana-ing—and generating—events.

onceptualized as an infrastructure, taking the length-ise stretch of its surfaces, the MEETT participates in strong and clear relationship with the territory while voiding its overt distortion. An infrastructure by its imensions and its staging within the landscape, upon approach, the MEETT reveals architecture of startling delicacy. Simple forms, light façades, smooth surfaces, precise details, the play of reflections and mirrors. All contribute to making the monumental nature of the facilities welcoming, its expressive power reappearing on several occasions.

The interior street that runs beneath the parking silo is the matrix of this new district. It is an essential structuring and functional element of the MEETT, an emblematic site of its urban character. Extending on both sides into the greater area, this axis will lead and organize future urban developments, albeit kept within controlled limitations. This "active strip," as defined by the architects, imposes its logic on the territory and simultaneously protects it from devastating urban sprawl.

From territory to architecture and *vice versa:* the MEETT is a stimulating reflection on the insertion of a monumental structure in an open environment, on the treasures of pure architecture contained in the modern era's large facilities, and on their capacity to be vectors of new forms of urban development. The project was fortunate to have met a project owner who was able to perceive within the drawings submitted for the project's competition the promises of a radical proposal. One who was able to accompany the plan throughout its development, allowing its initial ambitions to be preserved while respecting the project's given budget.

In 2011, boosted by an economic dynamic driven by aeronautics giant Airbus, the city of Toulouse launched the contest for a new exhibition center. Intended to replace an aging, unsuitable and impossible to renovate structure, the new facility had a twofold ambition. One, to furnish itself with facilities that meet international standards, enabling Toulouse to join the closed circuit of cities capable of hosting major trade shows, sporting, and cultural events. Two, to make this facility a new element and driving force of a space and aeronautics economic hub. The architecture contest set forth this dual perspective, with candidates not only having to define the architecture of the exhibition center but also having to propose an urban plan that organized the expected future developments around this strategic investment for the Toulouse metropolis.

The chosen site, to the north of the city, presented a situation that is unprecedented in Toulouse, a city marked by urban sprawl: an immense rural landscape stretching as far as the eye can see. The site was remarkably well-suited to accommodate the new facility, as it is near to the airport and Airbus' industrial facilities. On the other hand, it posed a real challenge to the architects: how to install a considerable aggregate of facilities through its easements and future developments without definitively altering the territory's qualities and perhaps even provoking a new phase of urban sprawl?

Reconciling the irreconcilable

It was precisely this program/site contradiction that would catch the OMA agency's attention, one of the three teams selected for the contest. It even contributed to a high level of interest and stimulation in the consultation phase. Reconciling the irreconcilable and making the improbable possible have often been the driving forces behind OMA's creativity. Reformulating the questions posed in radical, apparently irreconcilable terms is one of the strategies employed to bring forth new answers. In this case: implementing the requested facilities AND preserving the site.

OMA was to find the solution to this impossibility in the very nature of the facilities: their large scale. Not by denying or masking this dimension in more or less landscaped schemes, rather quite the opposite, by affirming, highlighting, and, one could say, by exacerbating it. Accommodating the territorial scale of the requested facilities would lead to radical, surprising proposals.

Density, a performance vector

The site was large, 350 hectares, but the requested program was considerable: 40,000 m^2 of exhibition halls that could be extended to 80,000 m^2, 40,000 m^2 of outdoor exhibition areas, a 15,000 m^2 hall to host major sporting or cultural events, parking spaces for 6,000 vehicles, not overlooking space for logistics, roadways, etc. . . . The banal and habitual activity of sticking small to-scale

quares representing the requested surfaces on a site lan would have been enough to display the incongruity f the convenient sprawl solution. Even less was it a ques- on of sterilizing seventy-eight hectares of farmland which would have remained empty most of the year) to ark thousands of cars.

ompacting and densifying was essential. As it was ardly conceivable to stack the exhibition halls one on op of the other (a solution that was out of economic each, but nevertheless explored), attention instead ocused on the parking spaces. Why not condense the arking spaces required for visitors in a silo car park? onsidering the additional costs, the concept was an conomic aberration, but arguments could be made in s favor. First of all, the environmental concerns, the soil conomy. But that was not all. The silo car park made possible to radically revise the traditional operations f an exhibition center. The often substantial distance etween parking area and exhibition halls disrupts func- onality. By positioning the silo car park close to the halls, his distance was eliminated. Visitors arriving by car were laced almost directly in the exhibition area. Density nproved the facilities' overall performance.

here remained to find the right relationship between he halls and the parking silo, and the positioning of the whole in a poorly structured site where the only point of eference was a departmental road. After testing nume- ous hypotheses, the simplest, most compact and econo- nical solution was chosen. The required surfaces were to e plied and condensed into three parallel strips: a hall or large events, a silo car park, and exhibition halls. By igning the requested exhibition halls, a 660-meter-long uilding was obtained. The silo car park was given the ame length, and the large events hall, extended by the ee exhibition area, formed the third strip. The territorial imension was upheld, and ground impact was reduced.

powerful gesture on territorial scale

his arrangement was to be the matrix of the urban roposal. Not a master plan—a formula long considered y OMA to be ill-suited to a rapidly changing world—but, gain, a strategy on the larger territorial scale. A long strip, the same width as the exhibition park (316 meters), extended from east to west on both sides of the park. This "active strip" was the focus of future development generated by the park. But it could also freely accom- modate sports and leisure facilities and installations. Density was combined with mixed use to design an urban plan that is open to the landscape. This continuous ribbon was also presented as a barrier against urban sprawl, a sort of urban cordon sanitaire intended to pre- serve the rural character to the north of the territory. OMA spared no expense in presenting its two proposals in order to speak to the jury's imagination: a superb scale model, a large-format presentation brochure, and suggestive visuals combining the International Paris Air Show and Luna Park to better underline the econo- mic and event-related potential of the facilities and the active strip.

While surprised, the jury was also captivated. The client intuited that the approach was not rigid, rather that there was plenty of room for maneuvering. If the fine- tuning process is inevitable in any project, it may as well be undertaken in concert with the preferred proposition.

And the story of the project's development would be that of the collaboration between an enthusiastic but res- ponsible project owner and a project management team that mobilized its immense research capacities to find compatible solutions related to functional requirements and financial obligations. From the outset, the opera- tional manager of the future facility would be involved in the decisive choices and would contribute their expe- rience with trade fairs and major conferences.

Questioning the program

A lengthy project development process began, which opened with questioning the program's scope. After the abandonment of the hypothetical 40,000 m^2 second phase, attention was focused on the size of the silo car park, the main additional cost factor. A very detailed study of the operation of the park would show that it was possible to reduce the number of spaces to less than 3,000. The financial savings were substantial. The physi- cal impact on the building was no less. The car park was narrowed from 72 to 33 meters width, reducing the entire project's footprint. At the same time, the access point for cars was revised. Initially imagined as a transversal car park with the complexity of a passage between the exhi- bition halls, it was moved to the west end. Located along the axis of the building, a 146-meter ramp leads directly to the first level, eight meters above ground.

Inevitably, the establishment of the exhibition park would lead to a review of the general road network in the area. In order to ease the already difficult local traffic flow, a two- by-two lane road was created along the park site connec- ting to the north-south departmental road. Eventually, this road was intended to become a new axis of entry to the city from the north, the construction of the exhibition center giving meaning to the construction of a new bridge over the Garonne.

Access for visitors on foot is from the east. A large, highly architectural forecourt forms the entrance to the MEETT and welcomes visitors arriving by tram. Guests then enter the exhibition grounds via a wide passage that slips gra- dually beneath the departmental road.

Structures: in search of savings

Designing an exhibition park means contemplating structure: covering large areas with a minimal number of load-bearing points and curtailed spending.

The silo car park is presented as a long concrete building with four levels based on a high ground floor (eight meters above ground). A giant mechanism of prefabri- cated posts and beams with an exceptional degree of precision ensured rapid assembly. On the upper floors, the reduction of the sections of the beams made it pos- sible to have largely ventilated parking with ample natu- ral lighting. The only elements providing a certain thea- tricality are the two large staircases and their escalators that lead visitors to the ticket pavilions. Access to the car park is free of charge, with visitor control at the entrance of the exhibition halls.

The inner street extends under the parking lot. Covered but open to the outside, it offers direct connections with the exhibition halls on one side and the convention hall on the other. It is the site of animation, punctuated by pavilions for ticketing, cafeterias, and rest areas.

The design of the large exhibition hall, 565 meters long and 82 meters wide, mobilized attention and research. Exchanges with the operational manager, but above all a permanent dialogue between client and architect led to many choices which, in addition to reducing costs, had a significant impact on the hall's final appearance, such as the free height under the frame, standardized at nine meters instead of the initially planned seven to twelve-meter variation. Or, along its sides, the installation of a base for services (bars, cafeterias, restrooms). Or the very innovative solution for ensuring separation between the halls with vertically retractable curtains that are housed in the structure's thickness.

For the roof structure, multiple solutions were explored: large-span concrete beams, a square steel structure, fiber-reinforced concrete elements . . . At the request of Rem Koolhaas, who is sensitive to the concept of preservation, the reuse of old abandoned industrial structures was even envisaged. Research was conducted to identify large empty industrial halls that could be dismantled and rebuilt on site. This led to the discovery of two monumental 50-meter high halls at the Marine Corps Air Station in Santa Ana, California. Visual tests were even presented to the client, however, the option did not succeed as public procurement regulations complicated its implementation.

In the end, a classic—and economical— three-dimensional steel ball structure was chosen. The entire structure is made up of square layers supported at the periphery by light tripod posts secured by bases and, in the center, by steel posts. The cap was specially designed to render maximum slenderness in the façade, which slides, detached, behind the structure.

The effect of lightness in the framework is remarkable. This impression is all the more evident as the polycarbonate envelope continues unbroken on all four sides. This possibility was only considered at a late stage and its adoption is a good indication of the quality of the relationship that had been established over time between the various collaborators. While the project was in the final drafting phase, the architects wanted to reopen the hall on all four sides by removing the two three-story buildings that closed the gables and occupied the logistics premises. They placed these on the ground floor, under the mezzanines, which were enlarged. Both client and operational manager were convinced by the significant architectural gain. The mezzanines compensated for the reduction in the ground floor exhibition area.
In its final configuration, the exhibition hall appears as a unitary space, a long volume with a clear geometry covered by an immense light sheet and bathed in the soft daylight emitted by its four polycarbonate sides. This 40,000 m^2 exhibition area can be divided into halls of variable configurations, allowing for hosting simultaneous trade fairs.

A magic box

A final radical change came at an even later date. While the building permit had been obtained for the entire project, the ambitious hall for major events had to be abandoned and a new project, focused solely on a convention center program, was drawn up within a few months. This new plan had to respect one major constraint: stay faithful to the initial project's envelope so as not to have to procure a new building permit, which would have delayed the delivery of the facilities by several months. Worth mentioning again, simplicity characterizes the structure. Tremendous 90-meter long, 6.6-meter-high steel beams cover an immense volume of 90 × 40 meters and 13.3 meters height. Divisible by a movable wall, the ground floor can accommodate up to 3,500 delegates. The meeting rooms occupy a mezzanine floor, with vertical circulation and services located in the north and south gables.

A rich repertoire of mobile elements turns this very simple volume into a huge magic box with narrow 6.6-meter-high sliding panels that can be moved manually, partitions that move vertically until they disappear into the framework, and movable bleachers . . . All enable multiple configurations. The east façade is entirely glazed and fitted with a monumental sliding door that puts the convention hall in direct continuity with the open-ai exhibition area. This further opens the domain to large events.

Spatial experiences

During its development, the project refocused on its fundamentals: compactness, volumetric simplicity, and linear organization. The high totems along the southern area contribute to marking the exhibition park's limits. The urban composition consists of three large regular prisms, two long and one shorter, simply juxtaposed and separated by long, narrow passages. This tensioning of two façades, only eight meters apart, generates a striking spatial experience over a length of 565 meters.

Two elements ensure coherence, the unity of the whole. One is the inner street. Located under the silo car park and extending along its entire length, it serves as the project's structuring axis. Providing access to the different spaces on either side, it is the place where the exhibition center bustles and comes alive. Moreover, through its extensions, it structures and organizes future developments in the larger territory.

The other is the characterization of each of the project's elements. The architects did not want to differentiate each program but rather sought to achieve a steadfast global logic by treating each component in a similar way. Thus, the concrete floor evoking urban spaces reads like a homogeneous surface unifying the whole site. In the same way, the linear, rasterized lighting systems are found in the convention halls, under the ceiling of the silo car park, in the entrances, and in the exhibition halls. The logic is further reinforced by the enveloping systems and their lightweight appearance: polycarbonate for the exhibition halls and convention center, fine polyester slatted frames for the silo car park.

The result is a certain neutrality of the whole that is tempered by surprising polychromy. Externally, no spectacular or marked elements disturb the serenity of these considerable abstract volumes. The interior, to the contrary, reveals very opposite atmospheres.

more sensory approach to the void has been pursued. ach building offers a particular spatial experience: the lmost airy lightness of the exhibition halls, the taut nearity of the levels of the silo car park, the feeling of a nonumental cavern in the convention hall.

he construction of a singular urban polarity

Vhile the exhibition park was taking shape, the client ushed a reflection on the economic pole that the MEETT as to develop in the proximity of Airbus.
he "active strip" concept proposed by OMA during the ontest was retained but with nuances in its application. f the same 224-meter width as the MEETT, the strip is ffectively extended on both sides. But the free layout f large elements suggested by the architects gave way o a more conventional approach. Developments are ocated on either side of an axis that is the extension of ne park's central street. To the west, structures with an ndustrial character will accommodate economic deve- opments. To the east, around the multimodal hub, a igher density is envisaged with tertiary buildings and uality hotels accompanying the convention center's ctivities. Beyond that, towards the Garonne, the active trip frees itself from the orthogonal grid organizing the istrict, making way for a more landscaped treatment hat enhances the presence of natural areas.

o the north of Toulouse, an economic dynamic is in notion based on ambitious urban and architectural oncepts that introduce breaks with routine notions. hrough its scale, oscillating between architecture nd infrastructure, the MEETT is participating in the onstruction of a singular urban polarity to the north of he metropolis.

minique Boudet, fomer director of the ench architecture monthly *AMC*, is an dependent architectural critic, curator, and iter. He is the author of *Jean-Marc Ibos and rto Vitart Architecture and the City* (Ambra 11), and *New Housing in Zurich: Typologies a Changing Society* (Park Books 2017).

enealogy of an Architecture

ean Attali

he opening of the MEETT marks a step in the long series f projects designed but rarely carried out by OMA in rance. Since the contest for the Parc de la Villette in aris (1982), the master plan for the Euralille district and ne creation of the Lille Grand Palais (1989–1995), their oluntary abstention from the site of the new city of lelun-Sénart (1992), its proposals for the development f the La Défense district (Zac Danton, 1989–1995; Mission rand Axe, 1991; Tour Phare, 2006; Signal project, 2008; rbanity study, 2008), not to mention, still in Paris, their articipation in international contests for the future rançois-Mitterrand Library (1988), the university libraries n the Jussieu Campus (1992–1993), and the renovation f the Les Halles district (2003), for a long period, Rem oolhaas and OMA, with the exception of the Lille project, vould not have built in France aside from their work for rivate clients (Villa Dall'Ava, Saint-Cloud, 1991; Lemoîne louse, Floirac, 1998).

lowever, recent years have seen the agency win and ring to completion several major public works pro-ects: the Alexis de Tocqueville media library in Caen 2016), CentraleSupélec on the Saclay Campus (2017), the imone-Veil Bridge in Bordeaux (under construction), and ne exhibition center in Toulouse, now completed (2020).

he Toulouse project, beyond its functional economy, the ogic of its establishment, its scales of proximity (or dis-ance) with the city, with its road junctions, with Airbus, nd with the countryside, is a work of architecture and rban planning of the first order. Its singular features nust still be identified based on the spatial and technical xpressions of its program and through the prism of)MA's characteristic design framework.

gency

'he influence and dissemination of OMA's professional ulture bear the mark of their inspirer, who is resolutely ttached to his dual profession as an architect and wri-er. The signature is first and foremost that of *REM*[1]—its restige is meant to reflect on each project. However, the agency's proposals, constructions, and publications now form a thick catalog, and the thread that links them is becoming more and more entangled. The intellec-tual, artistic, and technical sources of a production long identified with the eponymous figure of Koolhaas have been constantly nourished by collaborators, countless interlocutors, and contributions from partners. In the case of the MEETT, the project is signed by three of them: Rem Koolhaas, Ellen van Loon, and Chris van Duijn. The agency's collective culture is made up of a tightly knit group of theoretical proposals, formal figures, positions captured in the phases of project development and on-site construc-tion, and permanent interactions with public and private sponsors.[2]

The principle of cross-fertilization is at the heart of OMA's culture and its philosophy of globalization[3]: ideas germinate here; they flourish elsewhere. No other than a European architect could imagine such imperious buildings, such theatrical hotels; no other country than America or Japan could have the audacity to build them. This is one of the many paradoxes around which Rem Koolhaas' manifestos coil. It seems that the collective practice of the well-versed design agency is seized with vertigo in the tournament of urban and metropolitan cultures around the world.

Double bind

The agency's own culture finds the energy for its renewal in its transmission: from one project, one exhibition, one building site to another. Its intellectual and professional matrix is constantly being reformed under the pressure of opposing constraints in a double bind: the obligation to stand out, to avoid being trivialized or perverted by the trade-offs between clients' expectations, the stan-dardization of work sites, technical constraints, budget management—the obsession with signature. And at the same time, the increase in capabilities, the obstinate refusal of repetition, all necessitated by a basic conviction: the addition of intelligences is the principle, the multi-plying agent, the only breeding ground for creativity . . . Professional efficiency acquired will be all the more impact-ful as these understandings will have been developed in disparate cultures.

Concept

A global economy, the strict reduction of architec-tural detail in favor of an exacerbated expression of the concept, such was the position defended by Rem Koolhaas from the construction of his very first buildings. The Kunsthal Rotterdam (1992) not only renewed the typology of the exhibition center, it also brought its spatial dramaturgy to a climax. Traversed by a street, closed at its periphery but pierced by a narrow portal in the geometric center of the built volume,[4] firmly divided but rolled up on itself, uniting in its spatial chiasmus the courtyard and the garden, the building associated the frugality of its tectonic treatments with the profusion of its fragmentary ambiences. The Kunsthal led to the architect deserting one of his driving formulas: "No details, only concept."[5]

The same lapidary economy was seen in the launch, some two years later, of the nave of the Lille Grand Palais (formerly Congrexpo), carried out by Rem Koolhaas/OMA on the fringes of the Euralille center, which was designed according to the idea of an effective and spectacular spatial continuity between the program's three constituent elements (Zenith, Convention Center, Exhibition Fair). The building having been completed within the limits of an austere budget, it literally displays the modestness of its cost: one of the façades, facing the main entry routes into Lille (the railways and flyover space of the ring road), angrily touts its scanty amenity and its brutalism in the strictest sense of the word. The lesson has been learnt, that of architectural radicality, assumed all the way through to the final lights of the construction site having flickered off.[6]

Scale

The large scale of the exhibition grounds is a source of audacity for structural engineering and one of intimi-dation for architecture. When it comes to large halls, architecture is pushed towards a principled minimalism: the largest possible space but devoid of any obstacles; staging that is supposed to dazzle but is reduced to a game of escapism. Fewer columns, fewer posts, fewer partitions, even if the requirement is tempered or even contradicted by the obligation to divide the space according to the measure of each event and by the safety rules that impose confinement in the event of a disaster. The most elementary geometry harbors hidden conflicts. An exhibition hall, 565 meters long and 82 meters wide—some four-and-a-half hectares of available surface area—not counting the two parallel buildings, the horizontal silo car park for housing 3,000 cars, and the large convention hall that can be opened wide onto the outdoor esplanade; although its dimensions are not exceptional—other exhibition centers offer larger areas—the MEETT is contained within a very tightly outlined framework.

The concerns for spatial economy and for the reduction of floor congestion justified a system with an almost suprematist design. The three buildings arranged in parallel lines, leaving only two service corridors between them, attenuate the effect of mass in favor of a perception that is above all linear. From the outside, the perception of this unique dimension—without apparent depth, a vertical order barely perceptible through the gigantic green claustra that unrolls its seamless envelope over the four sides of the parking silo—magnifies the emptiness of the outdoor esplanade and increases the astonishment at the other emptiness as soon as one enters the exhibition hall: a length of which one cannot see the end, an incredible amplitude of coverage.

Triangle

The plan view of the MEETT's location leaves no doubt: the parallel lines of the exhibition hall, the silo car park, and the convention hall form a perfect triangle with Toulouse-Blagnac airport's runways. The geometric sharpness of the right angle is visible on a map . . . and while landing. The subliminal layout inscribes on the ground a vision of context enlarged to the dimensions of the metropolis.

Context

The agency's strategy is, no matter what has been said, to counter the trends of any giant building irrespective of context. The famous comment "*Fuck context*,"[7] a real trap set for critics, was merely the denunciation of architecture's blindness to the city from which it draws its substance. Beyond the evidence repeatedly provided by OMA's buildings, admirably open to the urban landscape and in osmosis with it, Rem Koolhaas' most explicit theoretical position on the subject of context was formulated during the polemics surrounding his project for the McCormick Tribune Campus Center in Chicago (2003). In a text that is less well known than those of his celebrated books,[8] the architect-writer recalls the demanding attention of Mies van der Rohe when he drew up the plan for the campus of the Illinois Institute of Technology.[9] Taken out of context, writes Koolhaas, Mies' architecture would be like a fish out of water. The author offers a dazzling vision of Mies' composition: architectural objects pass in the background, while the backdrop (Chicago's urban grid, its landscape of unlimited configurations) comes to the foreground. Such would be, in the almost *Gestalt* interpretation proposed by Koolhaas, architecture's very operation. The figure would only be intended to make the background happen; an antifigurative tension which, when applied to architecture, makes the object communicate with the entire landscape. Or, in the case of the MEETT: the revealer of Toulouse's great metropolitan site.

Columns

Frank Lloyd Wright had this farcical image to explain his conception of the balance of a structure: "Why," he asked, "don't you carry the floors like a waiter carries his tray, with his arm raised, resting centrally on his fingers?"[10] How could one not think of this image of raised fingers (rather than the palm and flat of the hand) when looking at the arborescent posts—each of which draws three planes in space—that support the three-dimensional structure covering the MEETT's exhibition hall? They do not support floors but line up to hold the edges of the immense lattice frame. They rest on the base formed by the service rooms on the periphery of the building, above which runs a mezzanine promenade. Their silhouette is outlined against the light coming from the length of the translucent façades that spread natural light into the hall space. Hands with raised fingers, each pulling one end of the white blanket stretched overhead: the columns appear as dancing figures[11] while they play off one another to make the heaviness of the plateau imperceptible.

Canopy

The inversion of values between the heavy (gravity) and the light (air, atmosphere) is one of the best-cultivated tropes of Koolhaassian poetics. Let us recall the Villa Dall'Ava and its bedroom resting on slender legs, diverting attention from the powerful pillars carrying a concrete beam hidden in the center of the composition, forming a swimming pool on the roof of the glass house. In the same way, the tree-like posts in the MEETT hall only participate secondarily in the balance of the structure, which is supported by the beam hidden in the plenum, in each of the sections that divide the lattice sheet. The astonishing decorum of these aligned columns enhances the metal canopy they help to support and make a double play with the polycarbonate curtain extended behind them, which encloses the building by modulating daylight and backlighting.

The figures of gravity and anti-gravity seem indefinitely transformable from one project to another, from one scale to another, they are mobilized here for the benefit of a floating and almost snowy vision of the roof. The sunlight, subdued by the translucent walls, makes the roof's few openings barely perceptible. Together, the iridescent glow and the graphic design of the luminaires recall the magic of the ceilings from which natural light alternates with the brilliance of electric lighting. Kunstha again, perfectly combined a flat roof, zenithal light in the manner of old sheds, fan-shaped dihedrals housing the luminaires, and a steel bracing tube streaking this artificial sky and crossing it horizontally as the topstitching to this governing theme. The MEETT's white latticework offers a completely different architectural solution, but not without bringing out, under the giant canopy of its exhibition hall, a reminiscence of Rotterdam. Proof that an *elementary idea*[12] in architecture blossoms and metamorphoses from one building to another.

Balcony

The convention hall asserts maximal neutrality. Dedicated to events of all kinds (congresses, conventions major shows, sporting encounters, political meetings . . .) it offers its spaces according to various configurations. Its height, higher than that of the exhibition hall, gives

. the profile of an airplane hangar, which is confirmed y the monumental portal, opening like a curtain on the orecourt.[13] The machinery of the sliding doors or partiions that can be lowered or raised mechanically undernes the similarity of the hall with the stagehouses of the reat operas, but without the pomp . . .

he interior volume includes first-floor rooms that are hemselves modular, with acoustics that can be revererant or muffled. These are the prescriptions of the rogram. Except that the space maintained under the mbiguous regime of its potential and generic assignnents reveals the aptitude for its own staging. A balcony ffers plunging views of the hall's floor and renews one of he architectural devices already used in Seattle (Seattle entral Library, 2004) and in Porto (Casa da Música, 2005). n Seattle, the center of the library is designed as an ntermediate space, red, dark, and deep like the heart of he building, suspended between the lower and upper loors of the reading rooms. This mid-water platform is ymbolically charged with all the questions that weigh n the future of the book. It is magnified by a spandel-free window separated from the void by a metal nesh, behind which the visitor contemplates the readers' ves like Wim Wenders' angels in Berlin . . .[14] A plunging iew, a balcony opening from the indeterminate to he proven. In Porto, breaking with the usual closure of oncert halls, the foyers open through high panels of orrugated glass to overhanging views of the perfornance in progress. The view from top to bottom and the istance imposed by the glass create a bubble of furtive olitude and temporary doubt about the meaning of the ollective demonstration. The message is implicit, it can emain unnoticed. But the reappearance of the motif n several of Rem Koolhaas' major projects keeps the bserver, the critic, on alert. We are once again close to he "Miesian" theme praised by the Dutch architect: "the usion of the sublime and the generic into a new hybrid."[15]

1. *REM* (75 mins, 2016) is the title of the film that filmmaker Tomas Koolhaas produced and directed about his father. See https://vimeo.com/ondemand/rem2.
2. OMA's professional structure is that of an international firm: seven offices around the world (Rotterdam, New York, Hong Kong, Beijing, Doha, Dubai, Brisbane), nine partners, 275 employees, forty-eight nationalities. See the agency's website: https://oma.eu/office.
3. See Rem Koolhaas et al., "Globalization," *S,M,L,XL*, 1995, pp. 363–369.
4. Kunsthal has been deeply renovated in 2013. Since its reopening in February 2014, the main entrance is now set up from the Museumpark.
5. See Alexandro Zaera Polo, "Finding Freedoms: Conversations with Rem Koolhaas," *El Croquis*, 53, 1992.
6. See Isabelle Menu, Frank Vermandel (eds.), *Euralille, Poser, Exposer, Lille, Espace croisé*, 1995. Partially reprinted in Christophe van Gerrewey (ed.), *OMA Rem Koolhaas, A Critical Reader*, 2019, chap. 9.
7. Rem Koolhaas, "Bigness," *S,M,L,XL*, op. cit., p. 502.
8. *Delirious New York* (1978, 320 p.), *S,M,L,XL*, (1995, 1,344 p.), *Content* (2004, 544 p.), *Project Japan* (2011, 720 p.), *Elements of Architecture* (2018, 2,528 p.).
9. Rem Koolhaas, "Miestakes," in Phyllis Lambert (ed.), *Mies in America*, 2001, p. 716–743.
10. Frank Lloyd Wright, *An Autobiography*, (1932) 1943, p. 192.
11. See Joseph Rykwert, *The Dancing Column. On Order in Architecture*, 1996.
12. *Elements of Architecture* (op. cit.) underlines the polymorphism of "elements," the variety of their typological and architectural expressions. The ceiling, the wall, the window, the roof may well exchange some of their functions (here, the penetration of light into the enclosed space), and this availability of elements shows their ability to enter into a game of permutations. The history of styles is disintegrating in favor of a combinatorial and systematic vision of the elementary components of architecture. The transformation of the same idea through projects that at first glance seem different is the application and the explanation of the idea.
13. In fact, the dimensions of this "hall" are much smaller than those of the neighboring aeronautics factory. The hall covers a ground area of one-and-a-half hectares. The ceiling height is 13.5 meters, far from the 46 meters in the Airbus workshops.
14. *Der Himmel über Berlin* (English title: *Wings of Desire*), film, 1987.
15. Rem Koolhaas, "Miestakes," op. cit.

Jean Attali, philosopher and professor emeritus at ENSA Paris-Malaquais (National Superior School of Architecture Paris-Malaquais). His teaching experience as well as his research have been dedicated to the mutations of city and large metropolitan areas.

hen Reality Tests Concept

ernard Vaudeville

nortly before the end of construction, I discovered and ured the future exhibition center in Toulouse. Above l, I retained an impression of the extreme simplicity of e architectural response: 155,000 m^2 gathered in three arallelepipeds laid on the alluvial plain, the silo car park, e exhibition hall, and the convention hall. Each is one ast block, experienced from both outside and inside. nis radicality is on the scale of this disjointed territory, alf airport infrastructure, half agricultural, which the roject attempts to restructure and reconcile with the ale of the very large events that the center will host.

ne architectural concept, strong and simple, is now o longer a concept. It has become built, functional, aterial buildings. Do the simplicity and strength of the oncept mean that its materialization was direct and ncomplicated? On the contrary: a project is not fulfilled e a carpet is unrolled. Here I would like to evoke this assage, this work, which ultimately led to the buildings valked through. From experience, when you build, verything is difficult, there is friction and deceleration verywhere while you constantly fight against inertia. ertia is the topography of the place, the nature of the oil, the laws of physics, all kinds of norms and regu- tions, programmatic requirements, technological nitations, economic restrictions, not to mention the ultitude of opposing personalities that contribute to e project. Paradoxically, the stronger and simpler the ea, the more difficult it is to negotiate with all these onstraints.

did not experience the history of this project's realiza- on. According to the stories, it seems to have been rich, omplicated, and at times trying: the opposite of a long, uiet river. However, this negotiation with reality should ot be perceived as a weakening or a betrayal of the chitectural idea. On the contrary, it is in this testing of e idea by reality that architecture resides.

vould like to share a few observations, a few details aptured during my visit, which bear witness to the technical choices that had to be made to achieve its ends and reveal the ingenious strategies implemented to overcome its obstacles.

The alluvial plain

One photo of the construction site struck me: it captures the highly technological metal-and-polycarbonate hull of the convention hall, already completed, lying on rough, uneven stony ground. This is the opposite of what is usually done, which is to make a clean, above-ground base before building the superstructure.

We are on a perfectly flat alluvial plain close to the Garonne: the ground is loose, and water is not far off. It even skirts the surface of the gardens neighboring the exhibition center. It was necessary to backfill up to 1.2 meters to lead rainwater to run off by gravity and to manage its storage in clever retention basins. This Dutch soil, with which the architects are familiar, forbids the use of basements and technical trenches. This is why all the technical components are suspended from the roofs—ducts, electrical wiring, plumbing, etc. This is also why the structures are placed at very precise points, without anchoring, on stakes that will seek bearing capacity at a depth of more than twenty meters.

Once the mobile cranes and large construction machinery finished their work, the ground was covered with a simple concrete slab as a finishing touch. This coating is continuous between outside and inside, both in level and material: this allows exposures to extend beyond the boundaries of the buildings and, conversely, welcomes heavy machinery into the buildings. This lack of demarcation, as well as the choice of concrete, places us clearly in the register of airport infrastructure—runways, airplane hangars. The territorial scale is affirmed.

Parking silo: assembling three levels

As in Holland, cars are parked high up on several levels. The waterlogged ground is one of the reasons for this, and there was a desire to avoid the sprawl of a surface-oriented car park. For many visitors, this parking silo will be the point of arrival and departure. It can be seen from a distance, and is accessed by a ramp in a facility not unlike that of the Roissy 1 terminal. In the OMA project, it becomes the backbone of the exhibition center.

It is a protracted structure, 565 meters long, designed as a "full," seamless building. As a result, views from both the outside and the inside are impressive. There are few single structures of this size in the world: bridges, tunnels, three or four skyscrapers. By way of comparison, the largest container ship is only half as long. The three parking levels are laid out across 140 concrete posts, evenly spaced ten-and-a-half meters apart. They are wrapped in an open, green grid made of polyester panels, which turns underneath. The mesh openings measure three centimeters.

Six hundred meters, nine meters, three centimeters, how can these three scales coexist? We find here a thread of reflection explored by the OMA agency for a long time, and subject of the famous work *S,M,L,XL*. In other words, how do you make an assembly of heterogeneous materials and products form a whole? To build is to fit together geometries of different scales, for example to create a façade with a complex pattern using simply parallelepiped bricks, or to make a dome by means of a skillful stereotomy of cut stones. A common strategy is to cut through joints, create buffer zones, embrace overlaps. Here, OMA has chosen a much more difficult path, to eschew joining seams despite the building's very large size. The result has a particular resonance, perhaps not perceptible at first glance, which generates depth and breadth in the work. A bit like the way a superimposition of harmonics enriches a note.

To achieve this, a great deal of ingenuity was required to compensate for the manufacturing imperfections of the polyester panels, to absorb the expansions and shrinkages of the concrete structure, and to plan systems and a strategy for adjusting the installation of its 4,855 panels. Indeed, the greater the difference in dimensions, the more difficult this becomes. One example of this challenge is Anish Kapoor's Cloud Gate in Chicago, a polished stainless-steel pebble that is forty meters in diameter with no discernible joints. In a more industrial register, we can also see a kinship with the development of continuous welded rail, stretching for miles without interruption. This apparent simplification required years of development and technological progress. It was necessary to invent new welding systems and new connections with crossties before it could be implemented on the rail network. One detail in particular reveals this work in the car park: the end of the parallelepiped where the three edges convene. The green mesh turns back perfectly without breaking. That is where the project's harmony manifests.

Exhibition hall: liberating the space

The exhibition hall is a 40,000 m^2 continuous space without partitions. The resulting interior display is striking. The building's main architectural objective is apparent: to provide possibilities, to render the fewest spatial constraints for future uses. It is reminiscent of the large hull of the CNIT in Paris, before its interior space was unfortunately colonized and re-divided. It also reminds us of the key argument of the Piano and Rogers project for the Centre Pompidou (also in Paris): return structure, technical equipment, and vertical circulation to the façade in order to completely free up floor space. But here, the scale is of a different order of magnitude since the hall's total surface area is equivalent to the sum of the Centre Pompidou's seven levels.

It takes a strong will and significant craftiness to free up space in this way. Today, there is a trend towards partitioning spaces, as this is the most obvious way of controlling and channeling phenomena and people. A recent example of this is the Parisian metro, where new automatic doors placed along the platforms transform them into corridors and abolish the perception of the stations' famous elliptical vaults. In the exhibition hall, the fire risk had to be managed, among other things. Regulations require the creation of compartments not exceeding 4,500 m^2. This is a major, unavoidable constraint, which generally requires the space to be intersected by fireproof partitions. Instead, the architects proposed "open areas," nine-meter-wide clear zones placed every fifty-eight meters, which can stop the spread of fire in the same way a firebreak path does in a forest.

These open areas provide rhythm to the space but do not close it off. The architects took advantage of this to group most of the essential hindrances that usually clutter up a space. In the roof, they created wide open-air trenches, like suspended backyards, invisible except from the sky, which allow smoke to be cleared from the hall. These concentrate the essential technical equipment, and each incorporate two large lattice beams, running from façade to façade. This is also where retractable curtains are placed, allowing the surfaces to be adjusted according to the events. The entire building's design derives from this organization. Between the open areas, thanks to the strategy of concentrating the technical functions, vast clearances form. To cover them, the architects used a mythical structural system from the 1950s/60s: the three-dimensional tubular-steel tablecloth, developed in particular by Konrad Wachsmann in the United States, the Mero company in Germany, Stéphane du Château and Jean Prouvé in France. Leaning on four sides, these structures are among the most efficient, allowing for immense reaches. The exhibition hall has seven of them measuring 54 m × 81 m, and a 81 m × 81 m square end sheet!

The hall's bracing system catches the eye with its elegance and simplicity. It consists of V-shaped tripods regularly placed along the façades, in exact geometrical homothety with the three-dimensional sheet. Here again, this device allows the central space to be freed of bracing cores or piers.

I am touching on many points of the exhibition hall's complexity, which have all been resolved with discretion, hidden from view. The building works, with all its functionalities and respecting all the rules, but what stands out are the immense emptiness of the hall, the simple regularity of the structures, the evaporation of the technical equipment, and the continuity of the translucent façades.

Convention hall: scenic machinery

The convention hall must be able to accommodate a more complex program than the exhibition hall: it will host conventions, conferences, shows, banquets, and exhibitions alternately or simultaneously, with all that is required in terms of comfort, acoustics, and services. Once again, the architects did not want to freeze its spatial organization. Flexibility is an OMA trademark. The building consists of a large hull of 156 m × 102 m, 20 m high, inside which unravels an astonishing scenic machinery made of removable partitions, retractable walls, retractable bleachers, and folding curtains.

The spaces can be reconfigured to best suit your needs in a very short time, as all this equipment is designed to allow for easy maneuvering. What makes the architecture of the place, beyond its vast volume, is this vocabulary of rails, bearings, cables, and motors like you would find in the backstage area of a theater, and also among the mobile bridges and port cranes of Rotterdam.

By culture, the world of construction is not concerned with mechanisms. Quantities of materials are moved during the construction process, and then immobilized, stacked and fixed for good. For example, structural calc lation, otherwise known as "statics," consists of checking that nothing moves in a structure, and especially that nothing moves for an extended period of time. The who regulatory and normative framework of the building is based on a principle of immobility, which means that when mechanisms are included in an architectural project, they are treated as incongruities, with differentiate procedures and specific guarantees.

Mechanical movement has been propelling its way into architecture for more than a century. The great achievement is the elevator, which paved the way for the skyscraper. The escalator and the conveyor belt followe However, when it comes to spatial transformations (partitions, roofs) by mechanics, there are far fewer examples: the pivoting floor of the Maison du Peuple by Beaudoin, Lods, Bodiansky, and Prouvé in Clichy, or the beautiful door mechanisms of the Maison de Verre by Chareau, Bijvoet, and Dalbet in Paris. More recently, economic necessity has led to the development of large scale mechanical systems: mega-doors for airplane hangars, retractable covers for stadiums. But in architectur the integration of mechanized movement is minimally ught after. OMA gives it another dimension by putting at the core of this project.

you walk through the three buildings, you experience e resolute desire to take advantage of what is techni-lly possible to open up new perspectives. This tenacity palpable. It allowed the original project's strongest ncepts to be carried through to the very end—into rea-y. This is remarkable because too many projects, which egin with very good intentions, falter under countless nstraints. On the other hand, technical solutions never hagocytize space, nor are technological innovations e main attraction. Technique is the underlying task, ut territory, humanity, usefulness, playfulness, and penness are at the heart of it all.

nard Vaudeville is an engineer and hitect, and professor at the École cionale des Ponts et Chaussées in Paris. s the founder and directing partner ESS engineering office, Paris.

otographs

In the life of an architectural project, its completion opens up a special period. After years of design work and construction, and before the client takes possession of the structure, the work is as if in waiting. Soon it will start operating and will deliver the performances expected by the client and envisioned by the architects. But for a while it remains still, silent, in the freshness of its completion.

This book wants to account for that particular moment and to show the project at the time of its completion. By its unusually large size and superb photographs, the book aims to reveal all the dimensions of an exceptional piece of architecture.

Our thanks go to Toulouse Métropole and Europolia. Their support has made the production of this book possible.

Our thanks go also to OMA office, which has supplied the photographs and contributed to the preparation of the book.

Project: MEETT (Construction of Toulouse Metropole new exhibition and convention center and its access facilities)

Program: Exhibition park and convention center

Site: Toulouse, France

Timescale: competition 2011, completion 2020

CLIENT

Client: Europolia – Société Publique Locale d'Aménagement de Toulouse Métropole & de la Région Occitanie

Project manager: Anne Fraisse

Team: Sébastien Dalle, Aurélien Taravella, Céline Letellier, Nadège Bergouts, Pascaline Guglielmi, Stéphane Sakubezak

Program: Menighetti – Jean-Claude Menighetti, Laure Gandon Neelson Accompagnement – Claude Eas

Construction economist: C2A – Bernard Richard

Environment: Franck Boutté Consultants – Frank Boutté, Florian Dupont

Building surveyor: Socotec – Philippe Salgues; Véritas – Vincent Damade

Planning: SCO – Marie-Christine Pons, Sandrine Leberre, Didier Rotelli

Ecologist: Ecotone

SPS: Veritas – Jean-Paul Otge

ARCHITECT

Architect in charge: OMA

Partners in charge: Chris van Duijn, Ellen van Loon and Rem Koolhaas

Contract manager: François Riollot

COMPETITION AND DESIGN DEVELOPMENT 2011–2016

Project architect: Clément Blanchet, Marcus Franck, Gilles Guyot

Team: Maria Aller Rey, Anton Anikeev, Adrian Auth, Polly Auyeung, Juhwa Baek, Henri Bardsley, Sara Bilge, Sandra Bsat, Denis Bondar, Kimiko Bonneau, Axel Burvall, Clara Cahez, Jorge Campos, Savinien Caracostea-Balan, Eugenio Cardoso, Lourdes Carretero Botran, Marek Chytil, Kaveh Dabiri, Solène de Bouteiller, Jan de Ruyver, Lionel Debs, Daniel Dobson, Francois Ducatez, Katerina Examiliotou, Peter Feldmann, Marcela Ferreira, Olivia Fontanetti, Nathan Friedman, Stavros Gargaretas, Matiss Groskaufmanis, Michalis Hadjistyllis, Chris Hayman, Didzis Jaunzems, Alexander Joksimovic, Anthony Joyeux, Matthew Jull, Eunjin Kang, Henri Kapynen, Agnieszka Kwiecien, Nicolas Lee, Laurence Lumley, Lawrence-Olivier Mahadoo, Sara Martinez, Elida Mosquera Martinez, Filippo Nanni, Thibault Nugue, Jamies Oliver, Pawel Panfiluk, Clement Perisse, Jerome Picard, Victor Pricop, Emmanouil Rentopoulos, Erik Revelle, Mario Rodriguez, Claudio Saccucci, Thomas Shadbolt, Michael Shafir, Hélène Sicsic, Jorge Simelio, Saul Smeding, Elina Spruza, Lukasz Skalec, Adrian Subagyo, Kyung Su Jung, Wes Thomas, Nicola Vitale, Chong Ying Pai, Haohao Zhu, Zheng Zou

CONSTRUCTION 2016–2020

Project architect: Gilles Guyot

Team: Kimiko Bonneau, Clara Cahez, My-Linh Dinh, Camille Filbien, Pierre Levesque, Hélène Sicsic, Nicola Vitale

Associate architects: PPA Architectures, Taillandier Architectes Associés

Partners in charge: Guillaume Pujol, Pierre-Louis Taillandier

Team: PPA – Jean-Michel Puig, Olivier Campayo, Charles Séguier, Quitterie Bourgela (Economic pole), Emmanuel Amalric. TAA – Foued Hammami, Emmanuel Peyrot des Gachons, Lucas Espeut (Economic pole), Stéphanie Loche PPA-TAA (chantier) – Jean Desfarges (Construction manager), Léonard Tiné, Eric Léger-Zheng, Vanessa de Castro Cerdà, Jules Terlaud, Minh Minh Le, Linh Nguyen

Engineers: Ingérop Conseil & Ingenierie

(Competition design development 2011–2016)
Project managers: Philippe Nanot, Pierre Alabsi

Engineers in charge: Laurent David, Vincent Beaudou, Florence Laumet

Team: Benoit Bobet, Christine Gabrielle, Anne-Sophie Pottier, Fabien Joly, Fabien Lasserre, Jean-Michel Conteau, Luc Gillen, Bruno Gerval, Laurent Rosolen, Dominique Gardeux, Denis Lasserre, Pascal Henquinet, Alain Leguillard, Daniel Verdier, Gilles Begouen, Stéphane Gourdin, Jean-Pierre Cœur, Diter Braet, Cyril Blachon, Vincent Achard, Frédéric Louit, Nabil Chakouh, Vivien Rosse, Orel Rivals, Philippe Castano, Marie Lafon, Christelle Garcia, Mélanie Clament, Sébastien Garcia, Matthieu Loup, Thomas Pauchet, Jean-Marie Amiable, Benjamin Robinet, Aimeric Desmoulins, Adrien Peyronnels, Taï-Phu Nguyen, Alberto Alonso, Raoul Gonzales, Marc Beaumont, Frédéric Gavel

Partners: Soconer, Ceryx, Efectis, Oteis, Vibratec

(Construction)
Project managers: Philippe Nanot, Patrice Boussaguet

Engineer in charge: Laurent David

Team: Yassine Verdret, Samir Id Brahim, Xavier Cance, Batouré Barmou-Batoure, Sébastien Varenne, Benoit Bobet, François Ramier, Matthieu Enaux, Patrick Nigou, Bruno Gerval, Philippe Soyez, Cyril Blachon, Philippe Castano, Vincent Achard, Vivien Rosse, Nabil Chakouh, Antony Delachaise, Laurent Saucet, Alberto Alonso, Sébastien Garcia, Diter Braet, Thomas Perarnau, Mireille Albert-Dorleac

Partners: Soconer, Gexia Conseil

Landscape architect: Batlle I Roig – Joan Roig, Simon Gabillard

Façade: Arcora – Clement Devergie, Jean-Pierre Cœur

Lighting: 8'18'' – Nicola Medinacelli, Solveig Pezin, Anne-Sophie Rollet

Ergonomics: Abilis – Sylvain Biquand

Acoustics: RHDHV – Theo Rijmakers, Nicole van Hout, Marieke Krijnen

Scenography: Ducks scéno – Gregory Aldea, Pierre Jaubert de Beaujeu, Lucie Leger, Isabelle Serré

Economy: DAL – Vivien Saetta, Gwenael Capitaine, Guilhem Becard

Signage: BASE design – Fumi Congan, Jonas Nicolin, Erwin de Muer

Sustainable development: Soconer – Étienne Bertaud du Chazaud

CONTRACTORS, INFRASTRUCTURES

General excavation: Malet – Agence Toulouse Sud (contractor), Eurovia Midi-Pyrénées, Razel-Bec, Guintoli

Traffic signage: Mozerr signal, Sud-Ouest signalisation

Primary stormwater system: EHTP (contractor), La Garonne, Sogea Sud-Ouest Hydraulique, Sogatrap, Socat

Dry and wet networks: Barde Sud-Ouest

Retaining infrastructure: Aximum

Civil engineering and roadworks on the terrain: Groupement Eiffage Route Sud-Ouest (contractor), Giesper, Inéo Réseaux Sud Ouest

Structural engineering: NGE génie civile, Guintoli

Landscaping: ID Verde

Street furniture: Mozerr signal

Street lighting: Barde Sud-Ouest (contractor), Bouygues énergies & services

EXHIBITION HALL AND SILO CAR PARK

Foundations, structural work: Eiffage Construction Midi-Pyrénnées (contractor), Demathieu Bard, Crespy

Waterproofing silo car park: Asten

Shell and core, exhibition hall: Eiffage Métal (contractor), SMAC, DL Garonne, CDS

Lifts and escalators: Otis

Plumbing, sanitary installation: Quercy Confort (contractor), Thermatic, Tunzini

Heating, ventilation, air conditioning: Quercy Confort (contractor), Thermatic, Tunzini

High-voltage works: Cegelec (contractor), Matéos Electricité, Socorem

Low-voltage works: Fournié Grospaud (contractor), Socorem

Metalwork: CARRE (contractor), Constructions Saint-Eloi

Partition curtains: GB Agencement

Façade silo car park: ITE Sud-Ouest

Railings: Correcta SAS

Central axis pavilions: Artel Société Nouvelle (contractor), CANCÉ, EMP

Partition: Massoutier et Fils

Suspended ceiling: Massoutier et Fils

Interior joinery: Coucoureux

Floor and wall coverings: Groupe Vinet

Painting: Groupement Roudié (contractor), Mozerr signal

Signage: Empreinte Signalétique (contractor), Videlio IEC, Fluo Néon

Fencing and gates: Correcta SAS

CONVENTION CENTER

Shell and core: Eiffage Construction Midi-Pyrénées (contractor), Demathieu & Bard, Crespy, Eiffage Métal, SMAC, DL Garonne, C

Heating, air conditioning, plumbing, electricity, lighting: Axima Concept (contracto Ineo MPLR

Glass partitions, metal doors, sliding door Constructions Saint-Eloi

Locksmith: CARRE (contractor), Constructic Saint-Éloi, Artel

Movable walls: Parthos France (contractor Parthos BV

Telescopic tribunes: Hugon

Interior joinery: GB Agencement

Lifts, escalators: Otis

Audiovisual infrastructure and event light Snef

Floor and wall coverings and painting: Roudié (contractor), Roudié Sol Français, Se Résine, Boeche Peinture

Partitions, suspended ceiling: Massoutier et Fils

Stage equipment: bc CAIRE

Products & equipment: Bardage façades polycarbonate–Arcowall Dott. Gallina SRL

Steel framing system, exhibition hall: Lani

Reinforced concrete precast double wall: F

Partition curtains: Solaris tende SRL

Polyester duckboard: Sous ATEX polyester renforcé de fibre

Lifts, escalators: Otis

Sliding panels: Forankra ACK SAS

Movable walls: Parthos

Industrial doors: Groupe DL

East and west façade, convention hall: Groupe DL

Sliding glass door, east façade, convention hall: Mineur Becourt

Telescopic tribune: Hugon

Media façade convention hall and signage Empreinte Signalétique, Videlio IEC, Fluo Néon